STAR WARS®
SHOWDOWN ON THE SMUGGLER'S MOON

STAR

WARS®

SHOWDOWN ON THE SMUGGLER'S MOON

Writer	JASON AARON
Artist, #7	SIMONE BIANCHI
Penciler, #8-12	STUART IMMONEN
Inker, #8-12	WADE VON GRAWBADGER
Colorist	JUSTIN PONSOR
Letterer	CHRIS ELIOPOULOS
Cover Art	JOHN CASSADAY & LAURA MARTIN (#7) AND STUART IMMONEN, WADE VON GRAWBADGER & JUSTIN PONSOR (#8-12)
Assistant Editor	HEATHER ANTOS
Editor	JORDAN D. WHITE
Executive Editor	C.B. CEBULSKI

Editor in Chief	AXEL ALONSO
Chief Creative Officer	JOE QUESADA
Publisher	DAN BUCKLEY

For Lucasfilm:

Creative Director	MICHAEL SIGLAIN
Senior Editor	FRANK PARISI
Lucasfilm Story Group	RAYNE ROBERTS, PABLO HIDALGO, LELAND CHEE

Collection Editor	JENNIFER GRÜNWALD
Assistant Editor	SARAH BRUNSTAD
Associate Managing Editor	ALEX STARBUCK
Editor, Special Projects	MARK D. BEAZLEY
Senior Editor, Special Projects	JEFF YOUNGQUIST
SVP Print, Sales & Marketing	DAVID GABRIEL
Book Designer	ADAM DEL RE

DISNEY LUCASFILM

STAR WARS VOL. 2: SHOWDOWN ON THE SMUGGLER'S MOON. Contains material originally published in magazine form as STAR WARS #7-12. First printing 2016. ISBN# 978-0-7851-9214-5. Published by MARVEL WORLDWIDE, INC., a subsidiary of MARVEL ENTERTAINMENT, LLC. OFFICE OF PUBLICATION: 135 West 50th Street, New York, NY 10020. **Printed in Canada.** ALAN FINE, President, Marvel Entertainment; DAN BUCKLEY, President, TV, Publishing and Brand Management; JOE QUESADA, Chief Creative Officer; TOM BREVOORT, SVP of Publishing; DAVID BOGART, SVP of Operations & Procurement, Publishing; C.B. CEBULSKI, VP of International Development & Brand Management; DAVID GABRIEL, SVP Print, Sales & Marketing; JIM O'KEEFE, VP of Operations & Logistics; DAN CARR, Executive Director of Publishing Technology; SUSAN CRESPI, Editorial Operations Manager; ALEX MORALES, Publishing Operations Manager; STAN LEE, Chairman Emeritus. For information regarding advertising in Marvel Comics or on Marvel.com, please contact Jonathan Rheingold, VP of Custom Solutions & Ad Sales, at jrheingold@marvel.com. For Marvel subscription inquiries, please call 800-217-9158. **Manufactured between 11/6/2015 and 12/14/2015 by SOLISCO PRINTERS, SCOTT, QC, CANADA.**

10 9 8 7 6 5 4 3 2 1

7

FROM THE JOURNALS OF OLD BEN KENOBI

“THE LAST OF HIS BREED”

WHILE SEARCHING FOR ANSWERS IN HIS QUEST TO BECOME A JEDI, LUKE SKYWALKER HAS UNCOVERED A JOURNAL WRITTEN BY JEDI MASTER OBI-WAN KENOBI, A JOURNAL THAT KENOBI SPECIFICALLY LEFT BEHIND FOR LUKE TO FIND. THE JOURNAL DETAILS KENOBI’S ADVENTURES DURING THE TIME HE WAS IN HIDING ON TATOOINE. WHAT FOLLOWS IS AN EXCERPT FROM THAT JOURNAL.

UGGGH!
TAKE IT ALL.
NO, PLEASE, THAT'S ALL THE WATER I HAVE TO SPARE.
YOU'RE A MOISTURE FARMER. FARM MORE.
BUT THE DROUGHT...IT TOOK MONTHS TO GATHER THAT MUCH. I NEED IT TO TRADE FOR FOOD.
PLEASE, I HAVE CHILDREN. YOU CAN'T DO THIS.
CAN'T?

MAYBE YOU'D LIKE TO COME TELL JABBA THE HUTT TO HIS FACE WHAT HE CAN AND CAN'T DO.
HMM?
NO?
DIDN'T THINK SO.
HHNGGH!
GLUG GLUG
WE'LL BE BACK TOMORROW TO COLLECT MORE TAXES!
UNTIL THEN...I SUGGEST YOU ALL GET BACK TO WORK!
AS HARD AS IT WAS TO BECOME A JEDI...

...IT WAS EVEN HARDER TO STOP BEING ONE.
BUT I DID.

BY THE TIME OF THE GREAT DROUGHT, IT HAD BEEN YEARS SINCE I'D TOUCHED A LIGHTSABER.
YEARS SPENT HIDING ON TATOOINE.

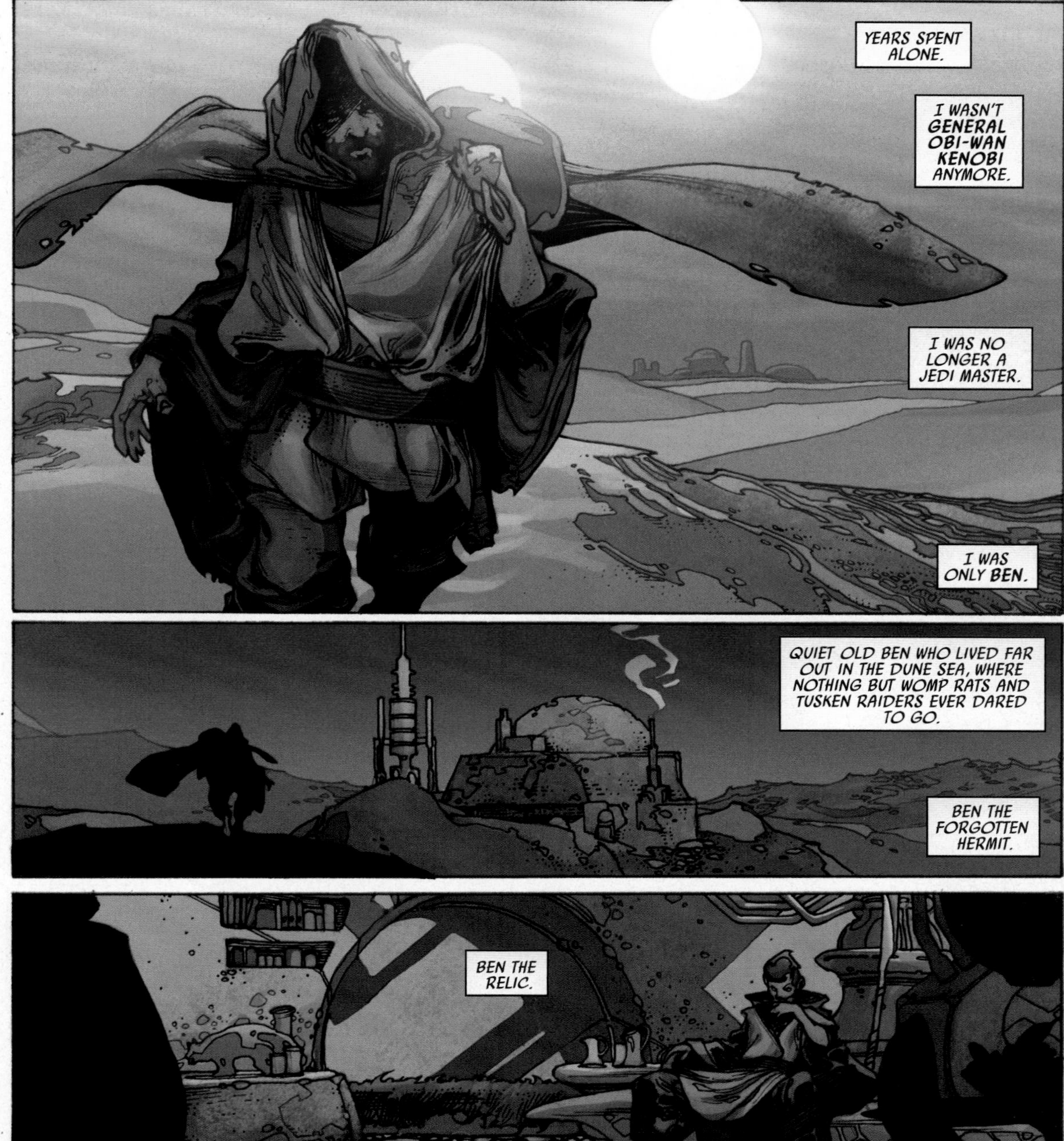
YEARS SPENT ALONE.
I WASN'T GENERAL OBI-WAN KENOBI ANYMORE.
I WAS NO LONGER A JEDI MASTER.
I WAS ONLY BEN.
QUIET OLD BEN WHO LIVED FAR OUT IN THE DUNE SEA, WHERE NOTHING BUT WOMP RATS AND TUSKEN RAIDERS EVER DARED TO GO.
BEN THE FORGOTTEN HERMIT.
BEN THE RELIC.

ONE DAY BLURRED INTO THE NEXT, WITH LITTLE TO DISTINGUISH THEM.
INSTEAD OF SITH LORDS AND BOUNTY HUNTERS, MY DAYS WERE SPENT BATTLING MONOTONY AND INACTIVITY.
I SHOULD HAVE BEEN BUSIER THAN EVER.
I SHOULD HAVE BEEN TRAINING THE BOY.
BUT HIS UNCLE NEVER ALLOWED IT.
AND I SUPPOSE THERE WAS A PART OF ME THAT COULDN'T BLAME HIM.
THE LAST SKYWALKER I TRIED TO TRAIN WAS GONE.
THEY WERE ALL GONE. ALL THE JEDI. AND SOMETIMES I WONDERED...
...IF I SHOULD HAVE GONE WITH THEM.

BUT I DID STILL HAVE ONE JOB TO DO.
AND I DID IT THE BEST I COULD.
VVVRROOOMM!!
WHOSE PLACE IS THIS?
THE LARS FAMILY. ACCORDING TO THE RECORDS, THEY'VE... NEVER PAID THEIR WATER TAX. HOW DID WE LET THAT HAPPEN?
WE'LL MAKE UP FOR IT RIGHT NOW.
TAKE EVERY LAST DROP.
WHAT THE...?

IT'S TOO HOT FOR DEATH WISHES, OLD MAN. MOVE ALONG AND DIE OF THIRST LIKE EVERYBODY ELSE.
YOU'VE TAKEN ENOUGH WATER FOR THE DAY. YOU SHOULD HEAD BACK TO JABBA'S BEFORE A DUST STORM COMES.
AND I SHOULD MIND MY OWN BUSINESS.
WE'VE TAKEN ENOUGH WATER FOR THE DAY. WE SHOULD HEAD BACK TO JABBA'S BEFORE ONE OF THOSE DUST STORMS COMES.
AND YOU SHOULD MIND YOUR OWN DAMN BUSINESS, OLD MAN.
IF I COULDN'T TRAIN THE BOY, I COULD AT LEAST KEEP HIM SAFE...
...AND HOPE THERE WOULD COME A DAY WHEN HE'D REALIZE FOR HIMSELF...
...THAT HE WAS MEANT TO BE MORE THAN JUST A FARMER.

IT WAS THE WORST DROUGHT ANYONE COULD REMEMBER.
THE MOISTURE FARMERS COULD BARELY GATHER ENOUGH WATER FROM THEIR VAPORATORS TO KEEP THEMSELVES ALIVE, LET ALONE TO TRADE IN TOWN FOR FOOD AND SUPPLIES.
ESPECIALLY WITH JABBA'S THUGS COLLECTING "WATER TAXES."
RUMOR WAS THAT THE BLOATED GANGSTER TOOK LAVISH BATHS ALL THROUGHOUT THE DAY, LEST HE PERSPIRE IN THE HEAT. BUT I DIDN'T BELIEVE THAT RUMOR.
I'D MET JABBA.
JABBA HAD NEVER BATHED IN HIS LIFE.
BUT IT WAS NO RUMOR THAT PEOPLE WERE DYING.
AND I WAS LETTING IT HAPPEN.
YOU NEVER TRAINED ME FOR THIS, MASTER QUI-GON.
YOU NEVER TAUGHT ME HOW TO FADE AWAY.

"ROCKS? YOU WANT TO SELL ME ROCKS?"
YOU MUST BE HEAT-CRAZED, OLD MAN. PEOPLE HERE NEED WATER. YOU CAN'T DRINK FROM A STONE. GET OUTTA MY TENT.
THESE AREN'T STONES. AND YOU CAN DRINK FROM THEM.
THEY'RE BLACK MELONS THAT GROW IN THE JUNDLAND WASTES. WHEN YOU CRACK THEM OPEN, THERE'S MILK INSIDE.
IT TASTES HORRIBLE, BUT IT'S SAFE TO DRINK. TUSKEN RAIDERS HAVE BEEN DRINKING THEM FOR YEARS.
YOU SHOULD TELL THE FARMERS THAT THEY CAN FIND THEM IN--
THERE THEY ARE!
YOU CAN'T KEEP TAKING OUR WATER! PEOPLE ARE DYING!
GO BACK TO YOUR FARMS! ALL OF YOU! OR YOU'LL WISH YOU HAD!
NOT WITHOUT OUR WATER!
YOU WON'T NEED WATER ONCE YOU'RE DEAD.
TAKE THEM DOWN.

THE GUNS ALL MISFIRED. AT THE SAME TIME? HOW IS THAT...
GET 'EM! TAKE THE WATER BACK!
I SHOULDN'T HAVE DONE THAT AND I KNEW IT. THERE WAS TOO MUCH AT RISK.
AFTER THAT DAY...
I DECIDED IT WAS BEST IF I DIDN'T GO INTO TOWN ANYMORE.

THERE'S A STRENGTH AND NOBILITY IN RESTRAINT.
I KNOW THAT'S WHAT YOU'D TELL ME, MASTER QUI-GON.
BUT NOTHING ABOUT THIS FEELS NOBLE.
THE PEOPLE HERE ARE DYING. WHILE I DO NOTHING.
I CANNOT FIGHT AS A JEDI. I CANNOT TRAIN THE BOY.
I AM LOST HERE, MASTER. LOST AND...

OH NO.

I COULD SENSE IT FROM ACROSS THE DUNE SEA.
WHERE IS HE, OWEN? I CAN'T SEE HIM ANYWHERE!
THE ONE JOB I STILL HAD LEFT...
I HAD JUST FAILED AT.
LUKE!
LUKE, WHERE ARE YOU?!?
WELL NOW.
WHAT HAVE WE HERE, BOYS?

I CAUGHT HIM TRYING TO STEAL WATER OFF THE SPEEDER.
THAT RIGHT, KID? YOU WERE TRYING TO STEAL JABBA'S WATER?
IT'S NOT JABBA'S. IT BELONGS TO THE FARMERS. I WAS TAKING IT BACK.
ALL BY YOURSELF, HUH?
I'M...I'M NOT AFRAID OF YOU.
HEH. YOU'RE A TERRIBLE LIAR, KID. WE'LL SEE IF YOU MAKE A BETTER SLAVE.
THROW HIM IN THE BACK WITH THE JUGS.

LIGHTS ALL BLEW.
YOU SURE YOU CAME ALONE, KID?
HUGGH?!
WHAT'S... SOMETHING GOT ME! I CAN'T...
WHAT'S DRAGGING HIM? THERE'S NOTHING THERE. THERE'S...
WHA... WHAAGGGGHHH!
THIS IS...HIGHLY IMPROBABLE.
THERE'S SOMETHING OUT THERE, PICKING US OFF ONE BY ONE! SHOOT IT!

OUTTA THE WAY, KID.
UGGH!
MY GUN...! I CAN'T HOLD IT! IT'S...
PERHAPS WE SHOULD HEAD BACK TO JABBA'S PALACE... JUST TO BE...
NO! WE STILL HAVE THE KID!
YOU HEAR ME OUT THERE?! WE HAVE THE BOY! STAY BACK OR WE KILL HIM!
I SWEAR TO YOU, I WILL GUT HIM LIKE A BANTHA AT--

BUT...BUT... HOW...
WE ONLY DID...WHAT JABBA...

AAHH!
HNNG!

UGGGHH

OWEN, HE'S HERE! LUKE'S HERE!
LUKE, ARE YOU OKAY?
WHAT...WHAT HAPPENED? HOW DID I...
THE FARMERS GOT THEIR WATER BACK. ENOUGH TO SURVIVE A BIT LONGER.
ABOUT A WEEK LATER, THE DROUGHT FINALLY LIFTED AND THEIR VAPORATORS STARTED CHURNING AGAIN.
JABBA WAS ENRAGED AND VOWED TO SCOUR THE DESERT TO FIND THE THIEF.
BUT NO ONE KNEW WHO HE WAS. NOT THE GUARDS HE'D BEATEN OR THE FARMERS HE'D HELPED.
NO ONE KNEW WHAT HE LOOKED LIKE.
NO ONE KNEW WHAT TO CALL HIM.

MY NAME IS OBI-WAN KENOBI.
THE LAST OF MY ORDER.
BUT THIS IS NOT THE END OF THE JEDI.
ALL IT TOOK WAS A YOUNG BOY'S COURAGE TO ASSURE ME OF THAT.
LET US HOPE THAT SOMEDAY SOON...I CAN TELL THAT BOY THIS STORY.

AND SO MANY OTHERS.
MIND STEERING FOR A LITTLE BIT LONGER, ARTOO?
I DON'T KNOW WHERE WE'RE HEADED, BUDDY...
WHRRRRP BRIP REEP
...BUT I'M WORKING ON IT.

Book II

SHOWDOWN ON THE SMUGGLER'S MOON

It is a period of renewed hope for the Rebellion. The evil Galactic Empire's greatest weapon, the Death Star, has been destroyed by the young rebel pilot Luke Skywalker.

But Skywalker knows he has a long way to go if he ever hopes to become a true Jedi. Seeking clues to his destiny, he recently returned to his home world of Tatooine, where he discovered a secret journal left for him by Jedi Master Obi-Wan Kenobi.

Meanwhile, Princess Leia and Han Solo have encountered some surprises of their own. While searching the galaxy for a suitable site for the new Rebel base, they ran afoul of Imperial patrol ships. Now hiding out on a remote planet, they find themselves facing a far more shocking encounter.

Her name is Sana Solo. And she claims to be Han Solo's wife....

An unnamed planet near the Monsua Nebula.
In an uncharted region
of the Outer Rim.
ATTENTION ALL STARFIGHTERS.
PATROLS REPORT THAT TWO HOSTILE VESSELS HAVE ENTERED THE PLANET'S ATMOSPHERE IN ORDER TO AVOID INTERCEPTION.
THE ATMOSPHERE IS RIFE WITH ELECTRICAL STORMS THAT HAVE SO FAR RENDERED OUR SCANNERS INOPERABLE.

ONE OF THEM IS AN IMPERIAL SHUTTLE WE NOW BELIEVE TO BE STOLEN.
NEVERTHELESS, WE SUSPECT THE SHIPS ARE STILL HIDING BELOW.
ALL TIE BOMBERS, COMMENCE BOMBARDMENT.
SET THE SKIES ON FIRE IF YOU HAVE TO, BUT FIND THOSE SHIPS.
AYE-AYE, CAPTAIN.
I LOVE MY JOB.
LONG LIVE THE EMPIRE!

Meanwhile, on the planet's surface...
WIFE?!
HAN...DID THAT WOMAN JUST SAY... THAT SHE'S YOUR WIFE?
SANA. WHERE DID YOU...HOW... HOW DID YOU...?
HOW DID I FIND YOU?
WASN'T DIFFICULT, DEAR. YOU'RE PATHETICALLY PREDICTABLE.
ALL I HAD TO DO WAS LEAVE A PROBE IN THIS PLANET'S ORBIT. I KNEW YOU'D TURN UP HERE SOONER OR LATER.
THIS SPOT WAS ALWAYS YOUR FAVORITE LITTLE RENDEZVOUS, WASN'T IT? OUR FAVORITE LITTLE RENDEZVOUS.
NOW, WAIT A MINUTE, THIS ISN'T WHAT YOU...

UGH!
WHAT A SURPRISE. YOU TASTE LIKE CORELLIAN WINE.
SHE'S A BIT SCRAWNY FOR YOUR TASTES, ISN'T SHE?
A WIFE. HE NEVER SAID HE HAD A WIFE.
BUT... SHE'S NOT MY--
YOU KNOW WHAT? THIS...THIS IS NONE OF MY BUSINESS. I'M JUST GONNA...GO. AND YOU TWO CAN...
YEAH.
SHE'S NOT MY WIFE! LEIA, WAIT...
"LEIA."
AS IN PRINCESS LEIA ORGANA.
I THOUGHT I RECOGNIZED YOU.

I'VE SEEN YOUR BOUNTY ALERTS. QUITE THE PRICE YOU'VE GOT ON YOUR HEAD.
SUDDENLY THIS IS ALL MAKING SENSE.
IT GETS EVEN BETTER. YOUR WIFE IS A BOUNTY HUNTER.
NO! AND SHE'S NOT MY--
THE RICH PRINCESS IN TROUBLE. YEAH, HAN COULD NEVER RESIST THOSE.
HOW MANY TIMES HAS HE RESCUED YOU? BET HE EVEN TURNED DOWN THE REWARD.
YEAH, HE'S HOLDING OUT FOR A MUCH BIGGER PRIZE.
AND EXACTLY WHAT SORT OF "PRIZE" WOULD THAT BE?
THAT'S ONE OF HIS BEST CONS. HE RAN THE SAME SCAM ON THE DAUGHTER OF A SULTAN IN THE BOZ PITY SYSTEM.
WHAT? NONE OF THAT IS TRUE!
REALLY? MAYBE WE SHOULD GO ASK THE SULTAN. I HEAR HE'S STILL OFFERING A MOON IN EXCHANGE FOR YOUR HEAD.
LEIA, DON'T LISTEN TO HER. IT WAS NEVER LIKE THAT.
NEVER LIKE WHAT? ALL A HUGE LIE? THEN WHY IS YOUR WIFE POINTING A GUN AT ME?
SHE'S NOT MY WIFE!
OH, REALLY? I HAVE SOME DOCUMENTS ON MY SHIP THAT SAY OTHERWISE. SHALL WE LOOK AT THEM TOGETHER?
WHY ARE YOU DOING THIS, SANA? WHY ARE YOU EVEN HERE?
BECAUSE IT'S TIME TO WRAP UP THIS LITTLE CHARADE OF YOURS, HAN. AND TIME TO COME--

THOSE ARE PROTON BOMBS.
THERE MUST BE TIE BOMBERS UP THERE.
YOU KNOW WHAT... MAYBE NOW ISN'T THE BEST TIME FOR THIS CONVERSATION. MAYBE WE SHOULD ALL JUST LEAVE.
OH, I INTEND TO.
IF YOU REALLY THINK YOUR HUSBAND'S WORTH KILLING SOMEONE OVER, MRS. SOLO, THEN BY ALL MEANS...
SHOOT ME.
NOW WHY WOULD I WANNA GO AND DO THAT, YOUR HIGHNESS?
COBRA, TARGET ONE AND FIRE.
LEIA, LOOK OUT!

YOU ARE EVEN CRAZIER THAN YOUR HUSBAND, LADY!
SANA, STOP THIS! WHAT DO YOU THINK YOU'RE DOING?
LIKE I SAID, HAN, YOUR LITTLE SCAM HERE IS FINISHED. I'M SURE IT WAS FUN WHILE IT LASTED, BUT NOW IT'S TIME TO CASH OUT.
SO HERE'S WHAT'S GONNA HAPPEN...
...WE'RE GONNA SELL HER ROYAL HIGHNESS TO THOSE IMPERIALS UP THERE.
AND THEN YOU'RE COMING BACK WHERE YOU BELONG, HAN SOLO.
BACK WITH ME.

STORIES.
I NEARLY DIED FIGHTING THAT BOUNTY HUNTER ON TATOOINE, AND ALL FOR WHAT? ALL BEN LEFT ME WAS A BOOK OF *STORIES*.
I DON'T KNOW WHAT I'M SUPPOSED TO DO WITH THIS. I DON'T SEE WHERE THIS BOOK TELLS ME *ANYTHING* ABOUT FIGHTING WITH A LIGHTSABER OR USING THE FORCE.
WE'RE RIGHT BACK WHERE WE STARTED, ARTOO. WHAT ARE WE SUPPOSED TO DO NOW?
TWEET BWOOP BEEDA BRIP
NO, WE *CAN'T* GO HOME YET. WE CAN'T GO BACK TO THE REBEL FLEET UNTIL I FIND SOME ANSWERS.
BUT YOU KNOW WHAT? YOU JUST GAVE ME AN IDEA.
THE *JEDI* HAD A HOME ONCE, TOO.

Nar Shaddaa.
The Smuggler's Moon.
WIP WIP WOOOO
YES, ARTOO, I KNOW NAR SHADDAA WAS NEVER THE HOME OF THE JEDI.
IT'S AN ENTIRE WORLD OF PIRATES AND OUTLAWS. IN OTHER WORDS...
...IT'S EXACTLY WHAT WE NEED.
ALL WE HAVE TO DO IS FIND THE WORST-LOOKING BAR AROUND. TRUST ME, ARTOO, I KNOW WHAT I'M DOING.
JUST LET ME DO THE TALKING.

AND BASICALLY THAT'S WHAT I'M... LOOKING FOR.
UM...
SO...
KILL HIM.
ROB HIM.
FEED HIM TO THE SCUM-SQUIDS.

NO, WAIT! I'M JUST LOOKING FOR A--
GAGGHH!
HRRGH!
BWOOP BWOOP EEEEP

THAT'S ENOUGH.
IS THAT A REAL...?
YES. YES, IT IS.
IT'S ME.
TELL THE BIG GUY I'M BRINGING HIM ONE.

WHERE DID YOU GET THAT WEAPON?
OH, SO **NOW** YOU WANNA TALK?
I CAME IN HERE TO CONDUCT **BUSINESS**, AND YOU TRIED TO **KILL** ME.
YOU'RE RIGHT, THAT WAS RATHER **RUDE** OF ME, WASN'T IT? YOU'RE OBVIOUSLY **NEW** AROUND HERE. LET'S START AGAIN.
WELCOME TO NAR SHADDAA. CAN I GET YOU A DRINK?
I TOLD YOU WHAT I WANTED WHEN I CAME IN HERE.
RIGHT. WHAT WAS IT YOU SAID AGAIN?
OH, YEAH.
YOU WANNA GO TO ***CORUSCANT.***

GIVEN YOUR CHOICE OF WEAPON, I'D GUESS YOU'RE SEEKING THE *JEDI TEMPLE*.
AND THAT YOU'D RATHER YOUR TRIP REMAIN SOMEWHAT... CLANDESTINE.
SO YOU NEED SOMEONE TO SNEAK YOU ONTO THE CAPITAL PLANET, PAST THE GREATEST CONCENTRATION OF IMPERIAL GUARDS IN THE GALAXY.
I CAN DO THAT. FOR A *PRICE*.
THE PRICE IS THAT SABER YOU'RE HOLDING.
THIS WAS MY *FATHER'S* LIGHTSABER.
THIS WAS MY FATHER'S *BAR*. BUT I'M GUESSING BOTH OUR FATHERS ARE DEAD, SO WHY DOES THAT MATTER? YOU WANNA GO TO CORUSCANT OR NOT?
I CAN GET YOU CREDITS.
I DIDN'T ASK FOR CREDITS. ALSO YOU'RE LYING. YOU'RE QUITE BAD AT IT.
NO DEAL. THE LIGHTSABER STAYS WITH ME.
THEN WE GO WITH THE ORIGINAL PLAN.
WE KILL YOU. WE ROB YOU. WE FEED YOU TO THE SCUM-SQUIDS.
AND I STILL GET THAT SABER.

YOU WANT THE SABER? COME AND GET I--
WHA?
THANKS.
DON'T MIND IF I DO.
GET THAT LIGHTSABER!

ATTENTION, BUCKETHEADS.
I'M ON THE PLANET RIGHT BELOW YOU. AND YOU'LL NEVER GUESS WHO I'VE GOT HERE WITH ME.
COME IN, IMPERIAL STAR DESTROYER. DO YOU READ ME?
SANA, WE REALLY OUGHTA...STOP AND TALK ABOUT THIS.
SANA?
YOU IDIOT. YOU SHOULD HAVE SHOT HER WHEN YOU HAD THE CHANCE.
TRUST ME, THAT'S NOT HOW YOU DEAL WITH THIS WOMAN.
ALSO SHE'S A BETTER SHOT THAN ME.
UNBELIEVABLE.
LOOK, I KNOW HOW TO HANDLE THIS, OKAY? JUST FOLLOW MY LEAD.
YOU TWO DONE WHISPERING?
SANA. HONEY. LET'S TALK. WE REALLY NEED TO TALK. PUT THE GUN DOWN AND WE'LL TALK, OKAY?
THIS IS ALL MY FAULT, I KNOW. I'M A SCOUNDREL, I ADMIT IT. BUT I PROMISE YOU I CAN...

WHU--
WATCH OUT, YOU IDIOT, SHE'S--!
GAAGH!
NOBODY MOVE.

LEIA?
THAT WASN'T EXACTLY THE PLAN, BUT OKAY, WE'LL--
I SAID DON'T MOVE, CAPTAIN SOLO.
I WASN'T JUST TALKING TO HER.
BUT...
WAIT, WHAT ARE YOU SAYING?
DID YOU REALLY THINK I WAS JUST GONNA STAND HERE AND LET YOU TWO SELL ME TO THE EMPIRE? THAT'S NOT HAPPENING.
HEH. HATE TO BREAK IT TO YA, YOUR HIGHNESS...
BUT YOU'RE ALREADY SOLD.
OH NO...

Nar Shaddaa.
The Smuggler's Moon.

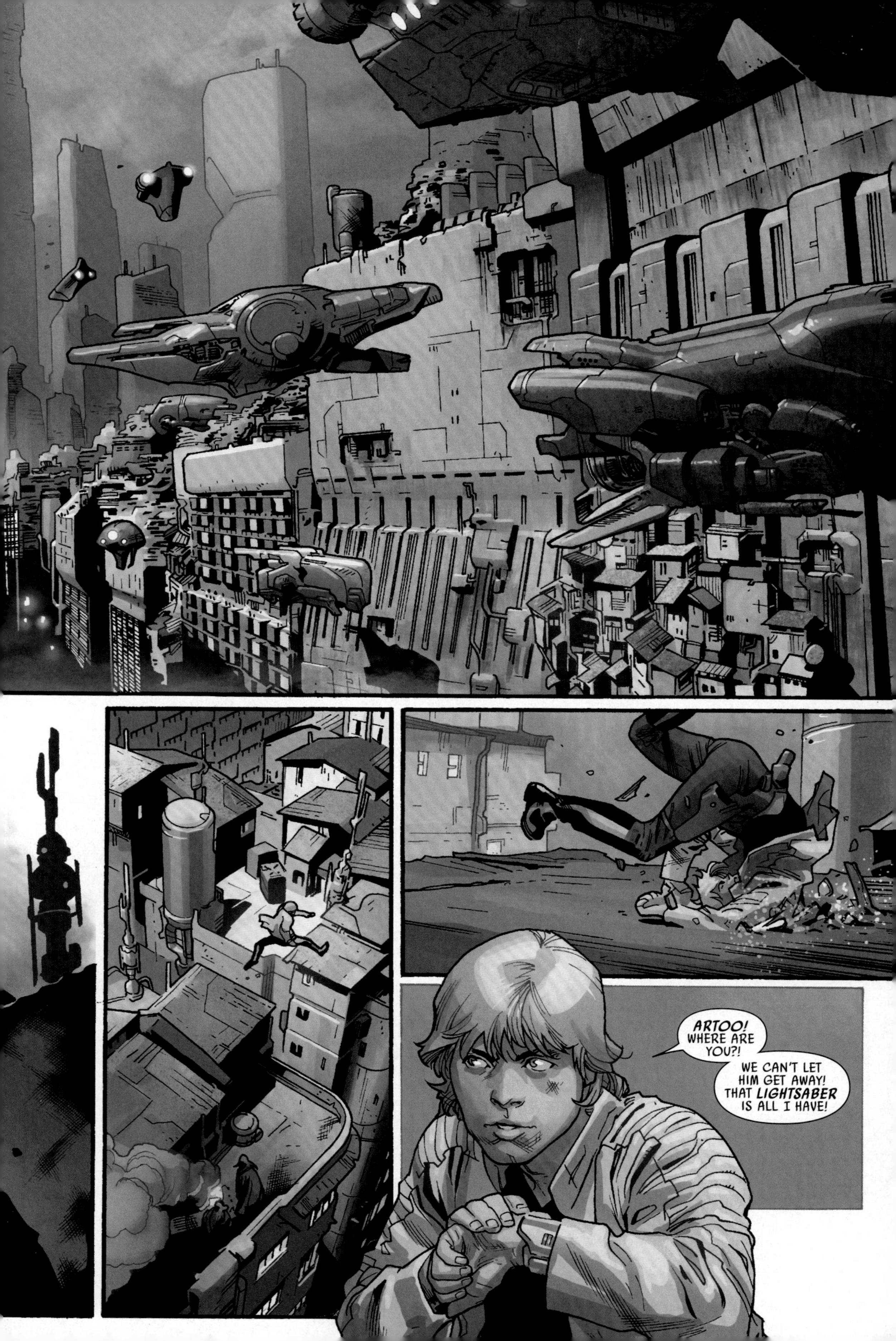
ARTOO! WHERE ARE YOU?!
WE CAN'T LET HIM GET AWAY! THAT LIGHTSABER IS ALL I HAVE!

NICE TRY, OFF-WORLDER! TOO BAD YOU ROOF-RUN LIKE A FARMER!
WELCOME TO THE SMUGGLER'S MOON! HA!
WAIT, WHAT ARE YOU...
DON'T BE A FOOL, YOU'LL NEVER...
WOOOO BLORP

GOTCHA!
GAAAGHH, YOU MANIAC! YOU'LL KILL US BOTH! GET OFF BEFORE THE...
AAAAAHHHH!

SHORTED OUT... MY MAGNA-GLOVE. YOU...HOW DID YOU JUMP SO...
YOU'RE INSANE.
NO.
I'M A SKYWALKER.
ARTOO...
THE OTHERS FROM THE CANTINA... LOOKS LIKE THEY STOPPED CHASING US. WONDER WHY THEY...
BECAUSE YOU'RE IN HUTTA TOWN NOW.

WHICH MEANS YOU AND THAT PRETTY LITTLE SABER OF YOURS...
BELONG TO GRAKKUS THE HUTT.
NOW PUT DOWN MY PROPERTY, BOY.
BEFORE YOU GET YOUR BLOOD ALL OVER IT.

An unknown world in the Outer Rim.
THIS IS ADMIRAL KEENER. TIE FIGHTERS, REPORT.
FIVE FIGHTERS WERE DESTROYED DURING ENTRY, SIR. THOSE STORMS WERE HELL. BUT WE HAVE THE TARGETS IN SIGHT.
APPREHEND... =KRRZZZT= AT ALL COSTS.
YOU'RE BREAKING UP, SIR.
I THINK WE GET THE GIST.
EVERYONE ON THE GROUND! NOW!
NICE KNOWING YA, PRINCESS.
BUT NOT REALLY THOUGH.
LEIA, WAIT, DON'T...

SANA, GIVE ME MY BLASTER!
I TOLD YOU, HAN. PLAYTIME'S OVER. WE'RE GOING HOME, LOVER.
WE'LL COLLECT THE BOUNTY ON HER LADYSHIP HERE AND RIDE OFF INTO THE--
YOU DON'T UNDERSTAND!
THEY WON'T JUST TAKE HER!
I'M A REBEL TOO!
YOU'RE A WHAT?!
I'M ON THE EMPIRE'S MOST WANTED LIST!
NOW GIVE ME MY DAMN GUN!
CONTACT. TARGET CONFIRMED AS THE TERRORIST PRINCESS, LEIA ORGANA.
GAAGH!
THIS IS A PRINCESS?
SHUT UP AND TAKE HER DOWN!

UGGGH!
JUST WHEN I THINK YOU COULDN'T POSSIBLY CAUSE ME ANY MORE GRIEF THAN YOU ALREADY HAVE... YOU MANAGE TO PROVE ME WRONG, HAN SOLO.
STAY BACK! BOTH OF YOU! I STILL DON'T--
WE DON'T HAVE TIME FOR THIS, LEIA! WE HAVE TO GO!
YOU HEARD THE MAN. GET ON THE SHIP, PRINCESS.
BEFORE I COME TO MY SENSES.

HNNRGH!

HOW DO YOU LIKE MY MAGNAGUARDS?
THEY'RE RELICS OF THE CLONE WAR. DESIGNED TO BATTLE JEDI KNIGHTS. OF WHICH YOU ARE CLEARLY NOT ONE.
FROM WHOM DID YOU STEAL THAT SABER?
HE SAID HIS FATHER WAS A JEDI.
WHY ELSE WOULD HE BE CRAZY ENOUGH TO WANNA GO TO THE JEDI TEMPLE ON CORUSCANT?
AND YOU BELIEVED HIM?
THE JEDI TEMPLE...?
HE'S EVEN MORE OF A FOOL THAN I THOUGHT.
I DON'T... I DON'T WANT TROUBLE.
NO?
THEN YOU CAME TO THE WRONG MOON.

ALL RIGHT, WAKE HIM UP.
DO YOU KNOW WHAT THIS IS?
WHERE AM I?
IN MY HOME. PLEASE ANSWER THE QUESTION.
NO.
NO, YOU WON'T ANSWER? OR NO IS YOUR ANSWER?
DOES IT REALLY MATTER?
I SUPPOSE NOT.
WHAT IS ALL THIS?
AH, THIS IS MY HOBBY. MY PERSONAL COLLECTION. THIS...

...IS ALL THAT REMAINS OF THE JEDI.
HOW... HOW DID YOU...
AS YOU MAY HAVE GATHERED, I AM NOT LIKE OTHER HUTTS.
YES, I CONTROL AN EXTENSIVE NETWORK OF SPICE SMUGGLERS AND BOUNTY HUNTERS. YES, I AM FRIGHTFULLY POWERFUL AND OBSCENELY WEALTHY.
BUT IT'S WHAT I DO WITH THAT MONEY AND POWER THAT SETS ME APART. I AM A COLLECTOR OF ANTIQUITIES.
THAT'S WHY YOUR AGENT STOLE MY LIGHTSABER.
YOU ARE HALF RIGHT. HE WASN'T JUST BRINGING ME YOUR SABER.
HE WAS BRINGING YOU.
THIS IS A JEDI HOLOCRON. ONLY SOMEONE WHO'S STRONG IN THE FORCE CAN OPEN IT.
YOU HAVE UNTIL THE COUNT OF FIVE TO DO SO.

WHAT? BUT I DON'T...
ONE.
I'VE NEVER EVEN SEEN ONE OF THOSE THINGS. I DON'T KNOW WHAT IT IS OR--
TWO.
HOW.... HOW DO I...
YOU CARRY A LIGHTSABER. YOU SEEK THE JEDI TEMPLE. FIGURE IT OUT.
THREE.
OKAY. OKAY, I'M TRYING.
I'M TRYING TO USE THE FORCE BUT I'VE NEVER...
FOUR.
WAIT. I CAN'T...
I...I...
BEN...
FIVE.
KILL HIM.

RECORDED HERE ARE THE TEACHINGS OF MASTER PHIN-LAW WO OF THE JEDI TEMPLE ON VROGAS VAS. PROTECT THEM AT ALL COSTS.
ANGER LEADS TO HATE.
THE CONSTRUCTION OF THE SABER MUST BEGIN WITH THE CRYSTAL.
ONCE WE WERE BROTHERS IN THE FORCE. BUT FROM THE HUNDRED-YEAR DARKNESS WERE BORN THE SITH.

TRUST ONLY IN THE FORCE.
WHOEVER IS SEEING THIS... IT'S UP TO YOU NOW.
DON'T LET OUR DEATHS HAVE BEEN IN VAIN.

DON'T LET THIS BE THE END OF THE JEDI.
WELL, WHAT DO YOU KNOW...IT APPEARS YOU WILL MAKE A FINE ADDITION TO MY COLLECTION AFTER ALL.
BUT...I'M NOT...
WHAT YOU ARE, DEAR BOY...IS THE LAST JEDI.
AND NOW YOU BELONG TO ME.
"TAKE HIM TO THE GAMEMASTER AND SEE THAT HE'S MADE READY FOR THE ARENA.
"AND THEN PREPARE TO RECEIVE OUR GUESTS.
"I EXPECT IT WILL BE QUITE THE PARTY."
BLIP BLIP BLURRRP

THEY'RE JAMMING OUR TRANSMISSION! I CAN'T CALL FOR HELP!
FORGET THE COMMS. JUST GET ON THE CANNONS AND KEEP THEM OFF MY TAIL. IF WE'RE LUCKY WE'LL LOSE THEM IN THE ATMOSPHERE.
IF WE'RE REALLY LUCKY, WE WON'T BE TORN APART BY THE STORMS. LET'S HOPE YOU HAVE BETTER TASTE IN SHIPS THAN YOUR HUSBAND.
IS SHE ALWAYS THIS CHEERFUL?
I REALLY THINK I SHOULD BE THE PILOT SINCE--
SHUT UP!
"WE'VE RECEIVED A DISTRESS CALL.

"FROM AN R2 DROID ON NAR SHADDAA.
"LUKE SKYWALKER'S R2."
IT APPEARS SKYWALKER HAS BEEN KIDNAPPED BY A LOCAL CRIME LORD. ONE OF THE HUTTS.
NAR SHADDAA IS THE LARGEST NEST OF OUTLAWS AND ASSASSINS IN THE GALAXY. WHAT WAS SKYWALKER DOING THERE?
WE DON'T KNOW. BUT THE BIGGER QUESTION IS, HOW DO WE GET HIM BACK?
I'M AFRAID THE HARD TRUTH IS...WE CAN'T. WE CANNOT MOVE IN FORCE AGAINST A HUTT, ESPECIALLY ON A WORLD LIKE NAR SHADDAA.
AND FOR A COVERT TEAM TO GO INTO SUCH A PLACE WITHOUT ANY MEANS OF SUPPORT....WOULD BE TANTAMOUNT TO SUICIDE.
I SIMPLY CANNOT GIVE THAT ORDER. NOT TO RESCUE ONE MAN. NOT EVEN ONE WHO SAVED SO MANY.
PLEASE FORGIVE ME, SKYWALKER.
NEITHER CAN I IMAGINE WHO AMONG THE ALLIANCE WOULD POSSIBLY BE BRAVE OR INSANE ENOUGH TO VOLUNTEER FOR SUCH A--
HHWWWWWWWWRR
I BELIEVE THAT ANSWERS YOUR QUESTION, CHANCELLOR.

RRRRRRRRRRRRRWWWWWWHHH
CHEWBACCA SAYS...WE SHALL LEAVE AT ONCE.
I BEG YOUR PARDON. "WE"?
OH, DEAR.

"HMPH. SHE MAY NOT LOOK LIKE MUCH OF A PRINCESS..."
...BUT SHE SURE SHOOTS LIKE ONE.
AND HERE I THOUGHT ONE SOLO WAS BAD. NOW I GET TO LISTEN TO TWO OF THEM. LUCKY ME.
HER NAME'S NOT SOLO! STOP CALLING HER THAT! SHE'S NOT MY--

LESS YAPPING AND MORE BLASTING, HUSBAND DEAR. OR THAT STAR DESTROYER'S LIABLE TO RUIN OUR HAPPY REUNION.
I'VE GOT A BETTER IDEA, SANA! HOW ABOUT YOU GET US OUTTA HERE?!
WORKING ON IT.
THE NAVICOMPUTER'S STILL PLOTTING OUR FLIGHT PATH. THEN WE'LL MAKE THE JUMP TO HYPERSPACE AND--
OH, NO.

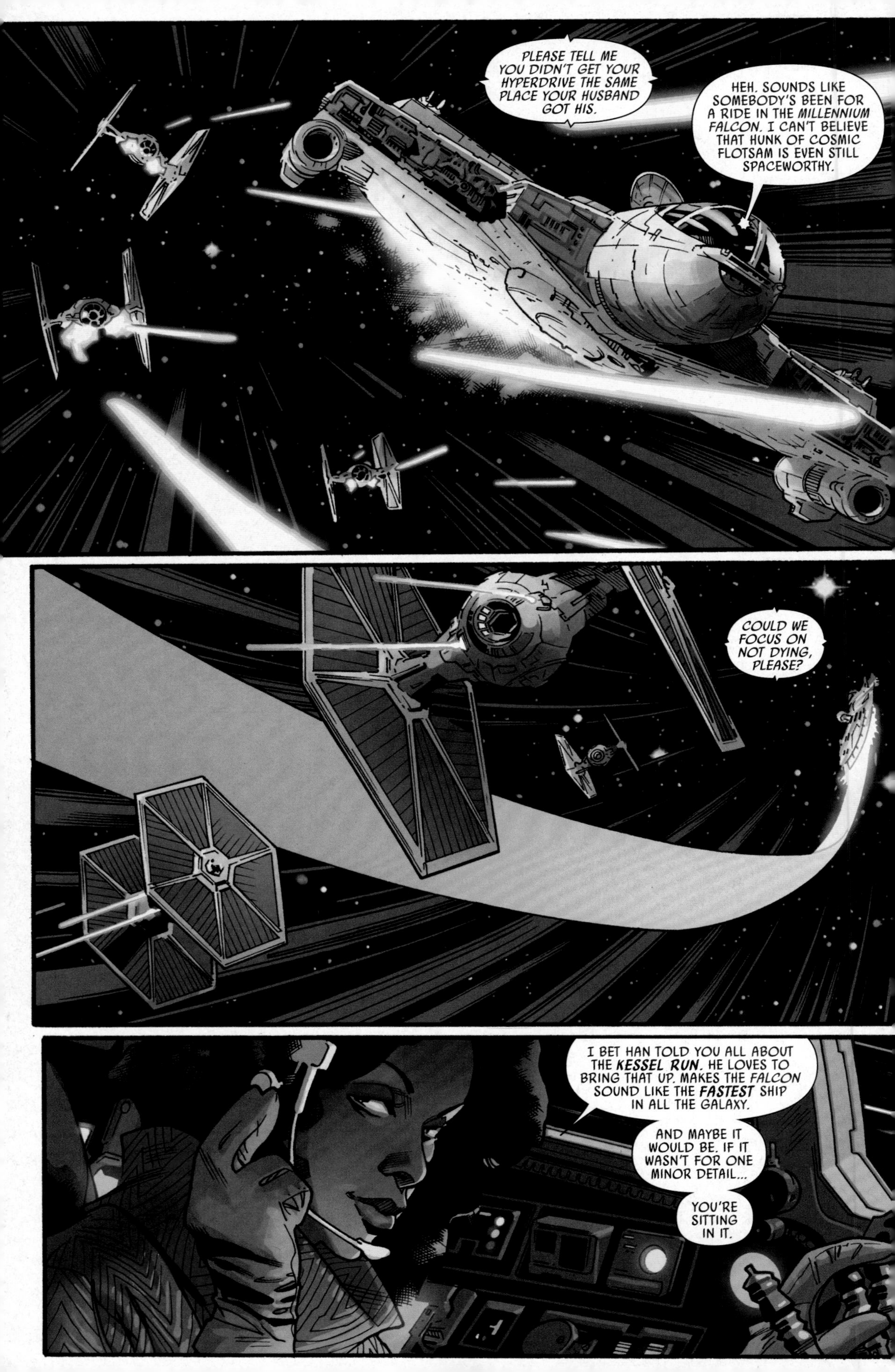
PLEASE TELL ME YOU DIDN'T GET YOUR HYPERDRIVE THE SAME PLACE YOUR HUSBAND GOT HIS.
HEH. SOUNDS LIKE SOMEBODY'S BEEN FOR A RIDE IN THE *MILLENNIUM FALCON*. I CAN'T BELIEVE THAT HUNK OF COSMIC FLOTSAM IS EVEN STILL SPACEWORTHY.
COULD WE FOCUS ON NOT DYING, PLEASE?
I BET HAN TOLD YOU ALL ABOUT THE ***KESSEL RUN***. HE LOVES TO BRING THAT UP. MAKES THE *FALCON* SOUND LIKE THE ***FASTEST*** SHIP IN ALL THE GALAXY.
AND MAYBE IT WOULD BE. IF IT WASN'T FOR ONE MINOR DETAIL...
YOU'RE SITTING IN IT.

WELCOME TO THE *VOLT COBRA.*
THE SHIP HAN *WISHES* HE HAD.

AND SAY *GOODBYE* TO THE EMPIRE.

NAR SHADDAA. I MUST SAY...
IT'S EVEN MORE REVOLTING THAN I IMAGINED.
HHRWWRRRRRGGH!
SAYING THAT YOU'RE MORE COMFORTABLE IN A PLACE LIKE THIS THAN IN A MEETING ROOM FULL OF PEOPLE IN UNIFORMS IS EXACTLY THE SORT OF THING THAT WORRIES ME ABOUT YOU, CHEWBACCA.
BUT GIVEN YOUR LEVEL OF COMFORT WITH SUCH LOCALES, I ASSUME YOU'LL HAVE NO PROBLEM LOCATING MASTER LUKE BY YOURSELF.
WHILE I STAY BEHIND TO WATCH THE SHIP IN CASE OF...
RRRRRRRRRRGHH!
WHY ARE YOU LAUGHING?
OH, I DON'T UNDERSTAND WOOKIEE HUMOR.
OH, DEAR.

THANK THE MAKER.
PARDON ME, MY FELLOW DROIDS. BUT I WONDER IF YOU MIGHT BE OF ASSISTANCE.
I'M SEARCHING FOR MY MASTER, WHO IS TRAVELING WITH AN R2 ASTROMECH, A THERMOCAPSULARY DEHOUSING ASSISTER WHO HAS A BIT OF A NASTY TEMPER AND...
SURE. WE'VE SEEN THEM. THEY WENT RIGHT THIS WAY. COME ON, WE'LL SHOW YOU.
OH, WHAT LUCK.
AH, THIS APPEARS TO BE A DEAD END. PERHAPS WE'VE TAKEN A WRONG TURN.
LOOKS A BIT SHODDY BUT THE JUNKERS MIGHT STILL GIVE US AN OIL BATH FOR HIM.
CUT HIS HEAD OFF SO WE DON'T HAVE TO LISTEN TO HIM YAMMER THE WHOLE WAY.
THESE DROIDS SEEM TO BE NOTHING MORE THAN COMMON CRIMINALS. TRUST ME, I AM AS SHOCKED AS YOU ARE.
PERHAPS WE SHOULD TRY ASKING SOMEONE ELSE?

HHHHRRRRRRGGHH!
WHU--
CHEWBACCA SEEMS TO THINK YOU LOT WILL SERVE HIS PURPOSES JUST FINE.
OH, MY. THAT'S RATHER...UNSEEMLY.
AH, TO REITERATE... WE'RE LOOKING FOR A FRIEND OF OURS.
ANY ASSISTANCE WOULD BE MOST APPRECIATED.
WWWWWWWWGGHH!

YOU MAY'VE OPENED SOME HOLOCRONS, BUT THAT DOESN'T MAKE YOU A JEDI.
I NEVER SAID I WAS ONE.
YET HERE WE ARE.
SO WHAT DOES THAT MAKE YOU?
THE MAN IN CHARGE OF MAKING SURE YOU PUT ON A GOOD SHOW WHEN YOU DIE.
YOU CAN CALL ME THE GAMEMASTER. BEFORE WE'RE THROUGH, I EXPECT YOU'LL THINK OF A FEW OTHER THINGS TO CALL ME.
I WON'T FIGHT FOR THE ENJOYMENT OF SOME HUTT.
YES, YOU WILL.

BECAUSE YOU WANT TO LEARN.
AND I CAN TEACH YOU.
NOT WHAT I NEED TO KNOW, YOU CAN'T.
THE JEDI TEMPLE ON CORUSCANT...
IT DOESN'T EXIST ANYMORE.
IT'S THE IMPERIAL PALACE NOW.
WHATEVER YOU WERE HOPING TO FIND THERE IS GONE.
ALL THE TEMPLES ARE GONE. JUST LIKE THE JEDI THEMSELVES.
FOR ALL WE KNOW, ALL THAT'S LEFT OF THEIR ORDER IS WHAT'S LOCKED INSIDE GRAKKUS'S VAULT.
THOSE HOLOCRONS... TOGETHER THEY CONTAIN ALL THE TEACHINGS OF THE JEDI. THE ANSWER TO EVERY QUESTION YOU COULD EVER POSSIBLY ASK.
IF YOU LIVE LONG ENOUGH, JUST MAYBE YOU CAN HAVE A LOOK AT THEM.

CUFFS OFF.
CATCH.
WHAT'S TO STOP ME FROM TAKING THIS AND...
ME.
AND ALSO *THEM*.
WE'VE GOT A ROOM BACK THERE FILLED WITH LIGHTSABERS. BUT EVERYONE WHO EVER USED ONE IS GONE, SO THERE'S NO ONE LEFT WHO KNOWS HOW TO KEEP THEM WORKING. EVERY DAY, MORE OF THEM SHORT OUT AND BECOME USELESS.
IF YOU'RE HOPING TO SAVE WHAT'S LEFT OF THE JEDI, KID...YOU'D BETTER HURRY. LET'S SEE WHAT YOU'VE GOT.

HUGGH
CONGRATULATIONS, YOU'RE ALREADY DEAD. AND HALF THE PEOPLE HAVEN'T EVEN FOUND THEIR SEATS YET.
GET UP.
AND NEXT TIME TRY A LITTLE *HARDER* NOT TO DIE.

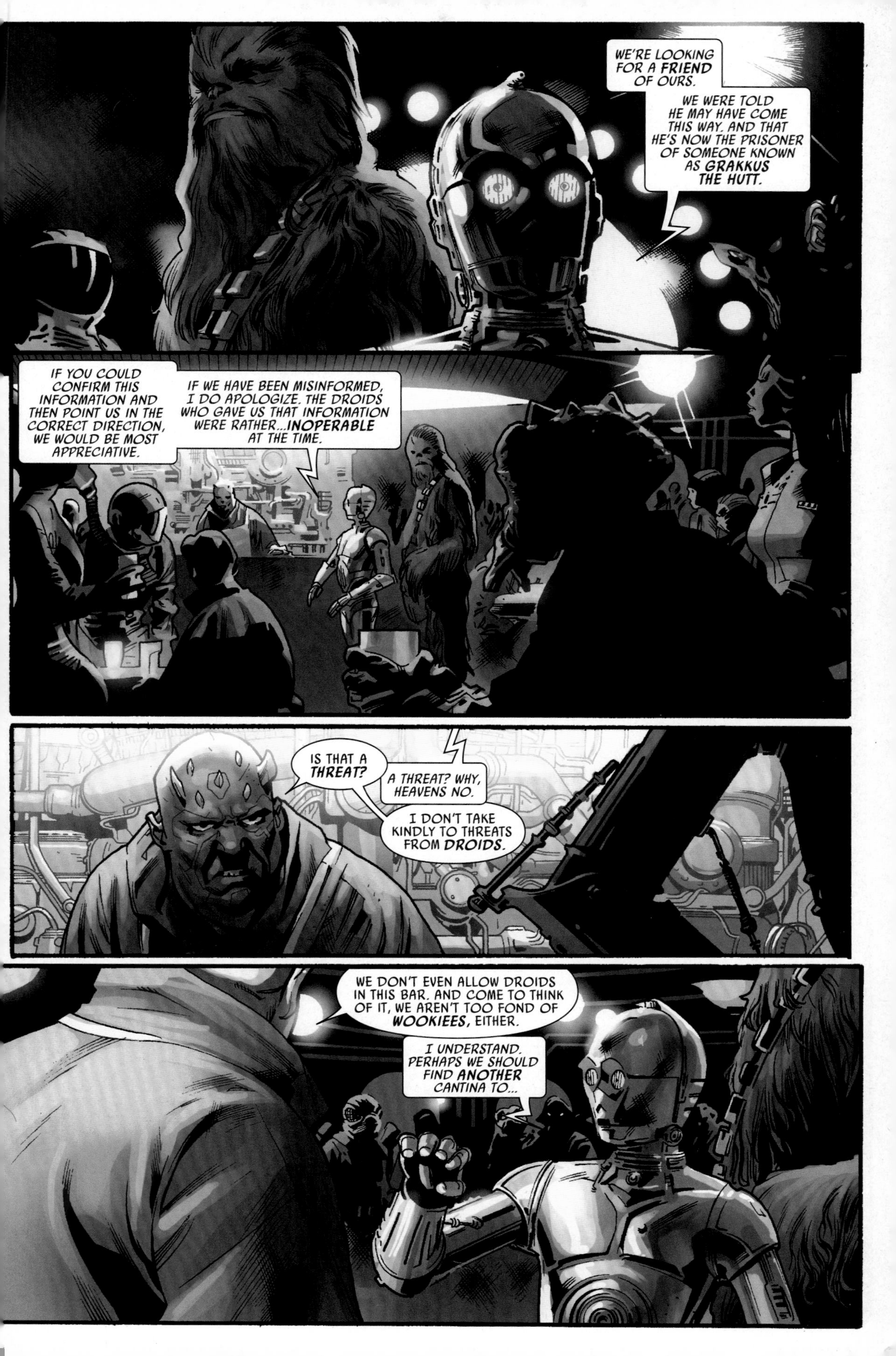
WE'RE LOOKING FOR A FRIEND OF OURS.
WE WERE TOLD HE MAY HAVE COME THIS WAY. AND THAT HE'S NOW THE PRISONER OF SOMEONE KNOWN AS GRAKKUS THE HUTT.
IF YOU COULD CONFIRM THIS INFORMATION AND THEN POINT US IN THE CORRECT DIRECTION, WE WOULD BE MOST APPRECIATIVE.
IF WE HAVE BEEN MISINFORMED, I DO APOLOGIZE. THE DROIDS WHO GAVE US THAT INFORMATION WERE RATHER...INOPERABLE AT THE TIME.
IS THAT A THREAT?
A THREAT? WHY, HEAVENS NO.
I DON'T TAKE KINDLY TO THREATS FROM DROIDS.
WE DON'T EVEN ALLOW DROIDS IN THIS BAR. AND COME TO THINK OF IT, WE AREN'T TOO FOND OF WOOKIEES, EITHER.
I UNDERSTAND. PERHAPS WE SHOULD FIND ANOTHER CANTINA TO...

WWWWRRRRRGGGHHH!!
CHEWBACCA SAYS...ANYONE WHO DOESN'T WISH TO BE... PHYSICALLY INCONVENIENCED SHOULD PERHAPS FIND ANOTHER ESTABLISHMENT IN WHICH TO CONSUME THEIR BEVERAGES.
AND THEY SHOULD DO SO...WITH SOME HASTE.
I SUPPOSE THEY DIDN'T UNDERSTAND. I'LL TRY ANOTHER LANGUAGE.

AND HOW IS MY JEDI COMING ALONG?
HE MAY BE STRONG IN THE FORCE, BUT AS FAR AS I CAN TELL, ANY TRAINING HE'S RECEIVED HAS BEEN CURSORY AT BEST.
WE DON'T NEED HIM TO DEFEAT DARTH VADER IN SINGLE COMBAT. ONLY TO DIE WITH SOME FLOURISH.
HE CAN DEFINITELY DIE.
EXCITEMENT IS ALREADY BUILDING. EVERY CRIME LORD ON NAR SHADDAA WANTS TO SEE THE LAST STAND OF THE JEDI. I EXPECT A PACKED HOUSE. YOU WILL HAVE HIM READY.
I ALWAYS HAVE THEM READY.

HAVE YOU DECIDED WHAT BEAST HE'LL BE FEEDING?
OH, NONE OF THESE PETTY LITTLE THINGS. NO, FOR THE LAST OF THE JEDI...
WE'VE BROUGHT IN SOMETHING SPECIAL.
MOTHER OF MOONS.
EVEN IF HE WAS A JEDI, I DON'T THINK HE'D LAST LONG AGAINST THAT.
EVERYTHING THAT HAS EVER LIVED HAS DIED IN MY ARENA.
EVERYTHING EXCEPT FOR A JEDI.
BLOOD AND LIGHTSABERS, MY FRIEND.
"THERE WILL BE BLOOD AND LIGHTSABERS."

"HAN SOLO, THE REBEL..."
AND HERE I THOUGHT MARRYING ME WAS THE CRAZIEST THING YOU'D EVER DONE.
IF I HAD MARRIED YOU, YOU'D BE RIGHT.
NO SIGN OF THE IMPERIALS. I THINK WE LOST THEM.
OF COURSE WE DID. THERE'S A SOLO AT THE HELM. DODGING THE EMPIRE IS WHAT WE--
ENOUGH OF THIS, SANA. WHY ARE YOU HERE? WHAT DO YOU WANT FROM ME?
SAME OLD HAN. YOU NEVER WANNA ADMIT WHEN YOU'RE CAUGHT.
WHAT'S NEXT, THE WHOLE "I THOUGHT YOU WERE DEAD" EXCUSE? OR ARE YOU REALLY JUST GONNA STAND THERE AND ACT LIKE OUR MARRIAGE ON STENNESS NEVER HAPPENED?
WE BOTH KNOW WHAT HAPPENED ON STENNESS AND IT CERTAINLY WASN'T A--
NAR SHADDAA.
WE HAVE TO SET COURSE FOR NAR SHADDAA.
I JUST TALKED TO THE REBEL FLEET.
LUKE'S IN TROUBLE.

NAR SHADDAA? WHY IS LUKE ON THE SMUGGLER'S MOON? WHAT WAS THAT KID THINKING?
TOO BAD FOR LUKE, WHOEVER THAT IS. BUT UNLIKE MY HUSBAND HERE, I HAVEN'T SUCCUMBED TO THE SEDUCTIVE WILES OF THE REBELLION.
WE'LL PAY YOU.
NO ONE'S OFFERING YOU AN INVITE INTO THE ALLIANCE. THOSE ONLY COME TO PEOPLE WHO EARN THEM.
BUT YOU'RE A SMUGGLER, AREN'T YOU? WHICH MEANS ALL YOU REALLY CARE ABOUT IS MONEY ANYWAY.
HEY, NOW WAIT JUST A--
I DON'T WANT YOUR MONEY, PRINCESS.
I JUST WANT MY HUSBAND BACK.
LEIA, JUST IGNORE HER AND TALK TO ME, OKAY? I REALLY THINK WE SHOULD ALL JUST STOP AND TALK ABOUT--
DEAL.
WHAT?!
AYE AYE, YOUR HIGHNESS. SETTING COURSE FOR NAR SHADDAA.

AAAAAGGHH!
I REALLY WOULD TELL HIM WHAT HE WANTS TO KNOW. HE'S QUITE UNREASONABLE WHEN HE'S LIKE THIS.
YES! GRAKKUS HAS YOUR FRIEND!
YOU CAN SEE HIS PALACE FROM HERE! IT'S TO THE EAST! JUST PAST THE SKYSLUMS!
I'M AFRAID I DON'T SEE...
TO THE EAST! EAST!
I SEE THE SKYSLUMS BUT...

HEH. YOUR FRIEND'S GONNA DIE IN THE HUTT'S ARENA.
IF YOU HURRY, MAYBE YOU CAN DIE RIGHT ALONG WITH--
AAAAAAAAAAHHHH!
OH, YES. THERE'S THE PALACE. I SEE IT NOW. IT DOESN'T APPEAR TO BE THAT...
WWWWWWWGHHHH!
WHERE'S THE BARTENDER?
YOU LET HIM GO?
OH, THAT WAS VERY KIND OF YOU.

"ISA HIM. MESA KNOW IT."
MESA SEEN HIM BEFORE. MESA PALO BEAT HIM AT DEJARIK, AND WELL, WESA JUST SAY...HESA MUI REGRETTING IT EVER SINCE.
ISA CHEWBACCA, MESA SURE. AND WHERE DAREE CHEWBACCA, HAN SOLO NEVER FAR BEHINDING.
JABBA STILL OFFER BOMBAD BOUNTY, YESA? MESA JUST FIGURED...MAN IN YOUS LINE OF WORKING MIGHT BE MUI GRATEFUL TO WHOSAEVER BRINGING DISA INFORMATION. OKEEDAY?
OH I'M GRATEFUL, ALL RIGHT.
THIS IS MY GRATEFUL FACE.
NOW WHERE DID YOU SAY YOU SAW THIS WOOKIEE?

"IMPOSSIBLE.
"THE PALACE OF GRAKKUS THE HUTT IS THE MOST HEAVILY GUARDED DWELLING ON THE ENTIRE SMUGGLER'S MOON.
"ESPECIALLY TODAY. EVERY CRIME LORD AND VILLAIN ON NAR SHADDAA IS COMING HERE.
"THE ODDS OF US SUCCESSFULLY INFILTRATING SUCH A PLACE WHILE REMAINING UNDETECTED...ARE 895 TO ONE. IN OTHER WORDS....
"...IT WOULD BE UTTERLY IMPOSSIBLE FOR ANYONE TO SNEAK INSIDE."

OH, POOR MASTER LUKE. I FEAR HE'S QUITE DOOMED.
HHHGGGGGGGH
YES, I KNOW I SAY THAT A LOT. PERHAPS IF EVERYONE LISTENED TO ME A BIT MORE OFTEN, WE WOULDN'T ALWAYS BE IN THESE SORTS OF--
GRRROOOOOGGHH
WHAT DO YOU MEAN, WE'LL FIGHT OUR WAY IN? THAT DOESN'T SOUND LIKE MUCH OF A PLAN AT ALL.
IF YOU ASK ME, THAT'S EXACTLY THE SORT OF RECKLESS BEHAVIOR THAT GOT ARTOO AND MASTER LUKE INTO TROUBLE IN THE FIRST PLACE.
OH, POOR ARTOO.
AND POOR US IF WE GO ANYWHERE NEAR THAT DEN OF DEATH AND...
RRRRRRRRGHHH!

HELLO, CHEWBACCA.
JABBA SENDS HIS REGARDS.
DEAR, OH DEAR.
WHERE'S SOLO?
NOT HERE. AND FOR THE FIRST TIME EVER, I VERY MUCH WISH HE WAS.
CALL HIM. TELL HIM DENGAR'S LOOKING FOR HIM.
HHHRRRRRRRGHHH!
MAKE SURE HE CAN HEAR HIS FRIEND IN THE BACKGROUND.
YES, SIR. IT'S JUST...
CHEWBACCA DID SAVE MY LIFE ON CYMOON-1. I SUPPOSE I SHOULD PROBABLY...
OH, WHY DO I ALWAYS HAVE TO BE THE HERO?
HEY, DON'T YOU--
HZZZZZZZZZZZTT

SIGH
CRAZY DROID. SHORTED OUT MY SHOCK BOLT.
WELL COME ON THEN, BIG GUY.
THERE'S A LOT MORE WHERE THAT CAME FROM.
RRRRRRRRRRRRRGGGHH!

READY FOR YOUR BIG DAY, MY BOY?
YOU'D BETTER BE. WE'VE GOT QUITE THE CROWD OUT THERE.
HE'S AS READY AS HE'LL EVER BE.
WHAT HAPPENS WHEN I WIN?
YOU JUST PUT ME BACK IN A CAGE AGAIN, RIGHT? AND FIND SOMETHING ELSE FOR ME TO FIGHT.
I WOULDN'T WORRY ABOUT ALL THAT. NO ONE IS PAYING TO SEE YOU WIN.
THEY'RE PAYING TO WATCH YOU DIE. TO WATCH THE FALL OF THE FINAL JEDI. DON'T DISAPPOINT THEM.
AND IF I DO? IF I REFUSE TO GO OUT THERE?
YOU STILL DIE. THOUGH MUCH MORE PAINFULLY.
AND I HAVE YOU STUFFED AND MOUNTED AND HUNG ON THE WALL IN MY MUSEUM. RIGHT NEXT TO THE OTHER JEDI RELICS.
RIGHT NEXT TO THIS.

THAT'S... HOW DID YOU...?
SOME SCAVENGERS FOUND YOUR SHIP. AND FOUND THIS HIDDEN INSIDE.
THE JOURNAL OF OBI-WAN KENOBI. ANOTHER FINE ADDITION TO MY COLLECTION. I THANK YOU FOR BRINGING IT TO ME.
NO!!! YOU CAN'T...!
SO FULL OF ANGER, THIS ONE. NO WONDER HE'S NOT MUCH OF A JEDI.
GIVE HIM HIS SABER.
THIS ISN'T MINE.
YOU WANT TO FINALLY BE A JEDI KNIGHT, KID? HERE'S YOUR CHANCE.
GO DIE LIKE ONE.

BEHOLD, THE LAST OF THE JEDI!
A VETERAN OF MANY GREAT BATTLES ALL ACROSS THE GALAXY!
SLAYER OF COUNTLESS HUTTS AND BOUNTY HUNTERS!
IT'S JUST SOME... BOY.
AND THE JEDI'S OPPONENT...FROM THE DOLOVITE MINES OF MUSTAFAR...
WHERE FOR YEARS HIS JOB WAS TO KEEP THE TUNNELS CLEAR OF XANDANKS AND GIANT MAN-EATING LAVA EELS.

H, I WAS PING IT WAS NNA BE THE TLE GREEN GUY.
DOESN'T LOOK LIKE MUCH OF A JEDI MASTER TO ME. MAYBE A PADAWAN AT BEST.
I'LL BET FIVE CRATES OF SPICE ON WHOEVER THE OTHER GUY IS!

--WHICH HE ENJOYED KILLING WITH HIS BARE HANDS.

GIVE A WARM NAR SHADDAA WELCOME TO THE LAST OF HIS KIND...
AND I THOUGHT WOMP RATS WERE BIG.

KONGO THE DISEMBOWELER!
GGGRRRRRRRRRROOOOOOOOOORRRRR
LET THE GAMES BEGIN!

LEIA...THIS IS RIDICULOUS.
I'M NOT GOING BACK WITH THAT WOMAN, I DON'T CARE WHAT DEAL YOU MADE WITH HER! SHE'S NOT EVEN MY WIFE!
I SWEAR, IF YOU'D JUST STOP AND LET ME EX--
SANA, I WANT TO KNOW AS SOON AS WE REACH NAR SHADDAA.
OH, TRUST ME, PRINCESS, YOU'LL KNOW.
AND THEN YOU CAN GET YOUR HIGH AND MIGHTINESS OFF MY SHIP.
GLADLY.
LEIA! LISTEN TO ME, YOU CAN'T KEEP...
DAMN IT! YOU WANT THE TRUTH?!
I MARRIED HER ON STENNESS!

OR PRETENDED TO MARRY HER, AT LEAST.
IT WAS ONE OF MY STUPID SCHEMES. TO GET BACK AT A CRIME LORD WHO'D BEEN DOUBLE-CROSSING SPICE SMUGGLERS.
HE OWNED A GAMBLING DEN. BIGGEST IN THE SYSTEM.
I PUT TOGETHER A TEAM, BUT WE NEEDED TO STAGE A BIG EVENT... TO COVER THE BREAK-IN. WE DECIDED ON A...
...A WEDDING.
AND IT HAD TO LOOK REAL. IT HAD TO PRETTY MUCH BE...
...BUT IT WASN'T...
...I MEAN, I NEVER ACTUALLY...
LEIA?
YOU GOTTA BELIEVE ME, I'M NOT...
AH, GREAT.
...I WISH CHEWIE WAS HERE.

GGRRRRRHH
I'M NOT JUST A PRETTY FACE, YOU KNOW. I CAN THROW A PUNCH AS WELL AS YOU CA--
HUUGH
OKAY, MAYBE NOT QUITE AS WELL.
BUT I'VE DEFINITELY GOT MORE TOYS.

UUH
HHGKK
KGGK. LIKE I SAID.
MORE TOYS.

HHHRRREEEEEEEEGH

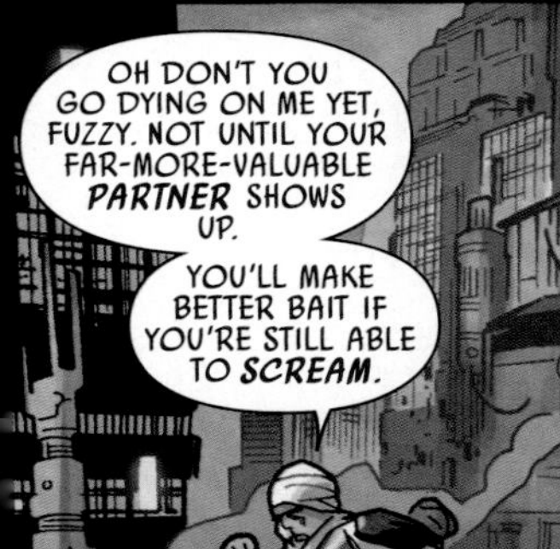

OH DON'T YOU GO DYING ON ME YET, FUZZY. NOT UNTIL YOUR FAR-MORE-VALUABLE **PARTNER** SHOWS UP.
YOU'LL MAKE BETTER BAIT IF YOU'RE STILL ABLE TO **SCREAM.**

YOU ***ARE*** STILL ABLE TO SCREAM, AREN'T YA?

MAYBE WE SHOULD CHECK, JUST TO BE SURE...

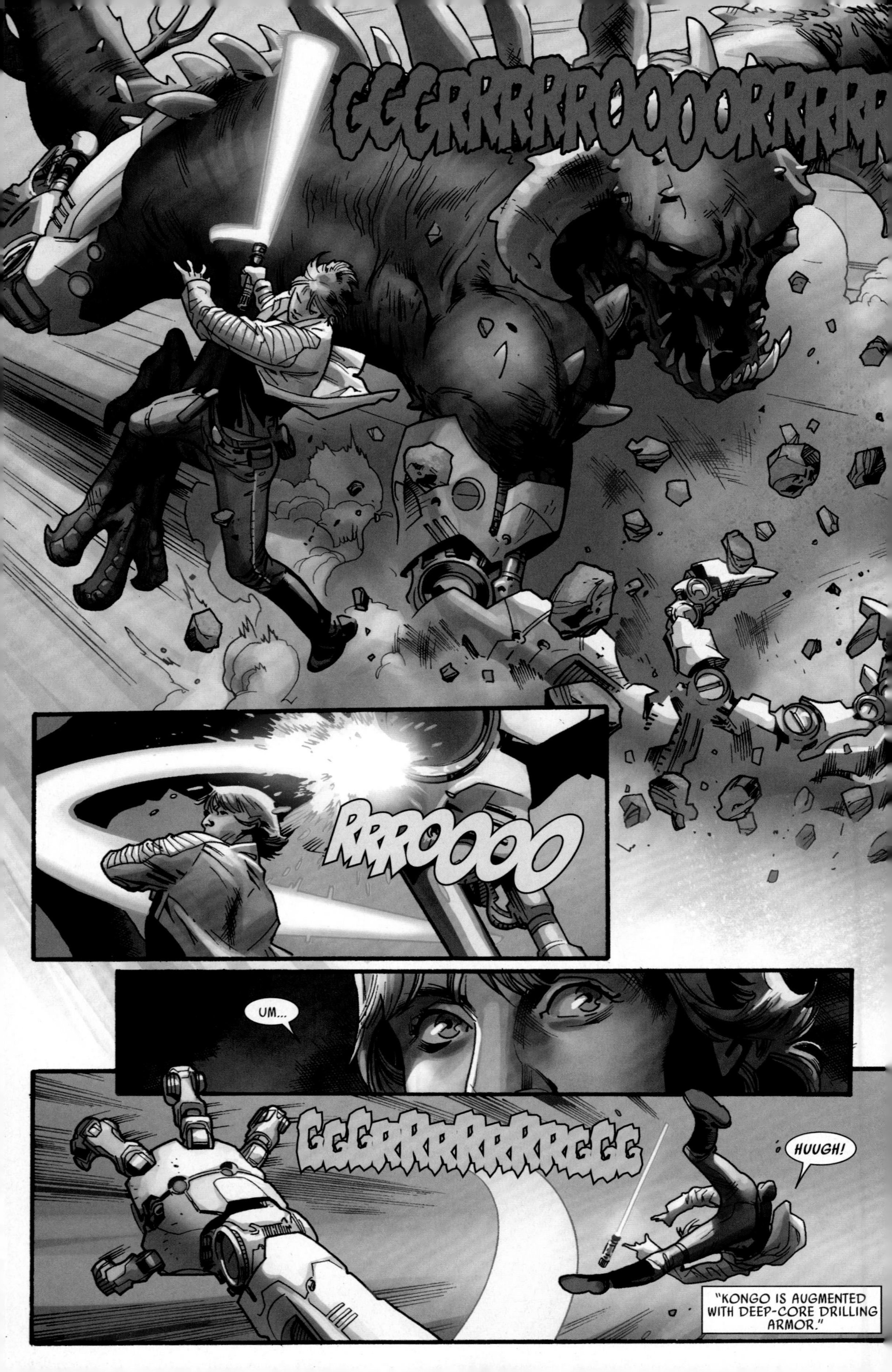
GGGRRRRRROOOORRRRR
RRROOOO
UM...
GGGRRRRRRRGGG
HUUGH!
"KONGO IS AUGMENTED WITH DEEP-CORE DRILLING ARMOR."

IT WON'T BE EASY TO HACK THROUGH THAT. NOT EVEN WITH A LIGHTSABER.
YOU SOUND ALMOST DISAPPOINTED, GAMEMASTER.
ON'T TELL ME AFTER ALL THE OOKIEES, LIZARD MEN, AND ACE PIRATES YOU'VE TRAINED D FIGHT IN MY ARENA, YOU'VE FINALLY TAKEN A LIKING TO ONE?
IT'S NOT MY JOB TO TAKE A LIKING TO ANYTHING.
HOW CORRECT YOU ARE. BUT WE ALL HAVE OUR WEAKNESSES, DON'T WE?
YOU WERE MINE, OF COURSE. THE GREATEST FIGHTING SLAVE I EVER BOUGHT. SO GREAT I COULDN'T BEAR TO WATCH YOU DIE.
MAYBE YOU THINK THIS BOY DESERVES THE SAME, BEING THE LAST OF THE JEDI?
TRUST ME, MY FRIEND, THE JEDI DIED A LONG TIME AGO. I KNOW. I OWN THE BONES.
BEST NOT TO LET DREGS LIKE THIS HALF-RAINED BOY LINGER ON AND SULLY THE LEGEND, EH? WOULDN'T YOU AGREE, GAMEMASTER?
GAMEMASTER?
THIS IS AGENT 5241. IF YOU WANT THE JEDI ALIVE, YOU'D BETTER HURRY.
COPY THAT, AGENT. WE ARE EN ROUTE NOW.

STAND BY FOR FURTHER ORDERS.
GGGRRRRROOO
I CAN DO THIS.
I BLEW UP THE DEATH STAR. I FOUGHT A BOUNTY HUNTER BLIND.
I JUST HAVE TO...TO USE THE FORCE. LIKE BEN TAUGHT ME.
JUST CLOSE MY EYES AND USE THE...
RRRHOOOOORRRRR
GAAAAGH!

OKAY, SO...
CLOSING MY EYES... DOESN'T ALWAYS WORK.
RRRRRRROOOOORRRR
WWOOOOWOOO WHEE

HHRRRGH
THE MIGHTY CHEWBACCA.
I MUST SAY... I EXPECTED BETTER. YOU HEAR SO MUCH ABOUT THE BIG, SCARY WOOKIEES. BUT YOU'RE REALLY NOT SO TOUGH AFTER ALL, ARE Y--
HNNNG!
YOU KNOW WHAT? MAYBE I DON'T NEED YOU SO ALIVE AFTER ALL!
JUST TELL ME ONE THING, AND I'LL PUT YOU OUT OF YOUR FILTHY, STINKING MISERY!
WHERE IS HAN SOLO?!

GAAAGH
RIGHT HERE, UGLY.
NOW TAKE YOUR DAMN HANDS OFF MY FRIEND.

YOU HEARD ME, DENGAR. YOU'RE OUTGUNNED.
SO STEP AWAY FROM THE WOOKIEE. AND I MIGHT JUST LET YOU LIVE.
THOUGH IF YOU'VE HURT HIM...
BETTER LISTEN TO HIM. HIS WIFE HAS AN ITCHY TRIGGER FINGER.
WIFE?!
I DON'T HAVE A...!
LEIA, WOULD YOU MIND NOT HELPING?
LAST CHANCE, BOUNTY HUNTER.
NO, IT'S YOUR LAST CHANCE, SOLO. IF I LET GO OF THIS THERMAL DETONATOR, WE ALL GO UP IN FLAMES TOGETHER.
SO HOW ABOUT YOU AND ME STEP ASIDE AND SETTLE THIS LIKE...
WHUGGH!

WAAAAGGGHH!
CONSIDER IT SETTLED.
CHEWIE, YOU ALL RIGHT, BUDDY? WHAT HAPPENED? WHAT ARE YOU EVEN DOING HERE?
WWWWRRGGHHH.
YEAH, WE'RE HERE FOR THE SAME REASON. WHERE IS HE, PAL? WHERE'S LUKE?
IS IT OVER? DID I...DID I JUST SAVE THE DAY?
SOMETHING TELLS ME...
...WE FOLLOW THEM.

GAAARGH!
DEATH TO THE JEDI!
KILL THE PRETTY BOY!
I WANNA SEE IT EAT HIM!
BEN! I COULD REALLY USE ONE OF YOUR MIRACLES RIGHT ABOUT...

SNZZZK
BOOOOO! I WANT MY MONEY BACK!
WHAT...? SOMEONE TRIGGERED THE BEAST'S SHOCK COLLAR. BUT I NEVER ORDERED...
WHO COULD'VE POSSIBLY...

GAMEMASTER? WHAT IN THE NAME OF NAL HUTTA DO YOU THINK YOU'RE DOING?!
SOMETHING I'VE BEEN WAITING YEARS FOR, YOU MISERABLE SLUG.
THE SHOW'S OVER, GRAKKUS. YOUR ARENA IS OFFICIALLY CLOSED.
OH, AND ALSO...
...YOU'RE UNDER ARREST.
THIS...THIS IS PREPOSTEROUS!
THERE HE IS.
MOVE AND YOU'LL WISH YOU HADN'T, KID.
WE'VE GOT HIM.
WE'VE GOT THE JEDI.

THIS IS SQUAD FIVE, MEETING SOME RESISTANCE IN THE SOUTH HALL.
JUST SOME DROIDS. NOTHING WE CAN'T HANDLE.
WHOOOO-OOOOOOO
WHRRP WHRRP WHRRRP

YOU FILTHY TRAITOR. YOU DARE TURN INFORMANT ON ME? AFTER EVERYTHING I'VE DONE FOR YOU?
ONLY A HUTT WOULD COUNT NOT KILLING ME AS A KINDNESS. AND I WAS ALWAYS AN IMPERIAL SPY, YOU IDIOT.
DID YOU REALLY THINK YOU COULD STOCKPILE A COLLECTION OF JEDI ARTIFACT THIS BIG WITHOUT THE EMPIRE TAKING NOTICE?
AND DO YOUR FRIENDS HERE REALLY THINK THEY CAN COME IN FORCE TO THE SMUGGLER'S MOON AND EXPECT TO LEAVE ALIVE?
ONE WORD FROM ME, AND THIS CROWD WILL TEAR THEM TO PIECES.
IF ANYONE DIES, TRUST ME, GRAKKUS, YOU'LL BE THE FIRST.
I TRUSTED YOU, YES, AND THAT WAS MY MISTAKE.
BUT YOU WERE STILL A SLAVE. I NEVER TOLD YOU ALL OF MY SECRETS. FOR EXAMPLE...
...TRIGGER ARENA PROTOCOLS, GRAKKUS FIVE.
VOICE RECOGNIZED. TRIGGERING NOW.

WHAT THE BLAZES...
A LOCALIZED E.M.P. BLASTERS ARE USELESS.
GET BACK. REGROUP OUTSIDE.
WHAT? WHAT ARE YOU, CRAZY? WE DON'T NEED BLASTERS TO TAKE DOWN ONE FAT, OLD--
WHU--!
WHHRRRGGHHAAAAAAH!
GRAKKUS ISN'T LIKE OTHER HUTTS.
THE MOST DANGEROUS THING IN GRAKKUS'S ARENA ISN'T SOME SAVAGE BEAST OR MINDLESS MONSTER.
YOU SHOULD'VE WARNED THEM, GAMEMASTER. NOW THEY'LL LEARN THE HARD WAY.
IT'S GRAKKUS.

TWENTY CREDITS ON GRAKKUS!
I'LL BET HE TEARS THE NEXT BUCKETHEAD IN HALF!
FIFTY CREDITS SAYS HE EATS ONE!
WE NEED BACKUP! COME IN!
YOU IDIOT, THE E.M.P. SHORTED OUT THE COMMS JUST LIKE IT DID THE...
RRRRRRROOOORRRRR
LIKE IT DID THE MONSTER'S CONTROL COLLAR!

GRAB THE KID! DON'T LOSE THE JEDI!
HOW MANY TIMES DO I HAVE TO SAY IT? I'M NO...
WHEE WOO WER WOO
THANKS, ARTOO.
SORRY, SO WHAT WERE WE TALKING ABOUT?

ALL THE GUARDS ARE DOWN. NOT SURE IF THAT'S A GOOD SIGN OR A BAD ONE.
THAT IS DEFINITELY A BAD ONE.
IF WE GET SEPARATED, MEET BACK AT THE *FALCON!*
YOU'RE NOT GETTING SEPARATED FROM ME, HAN SOLO! DON'T EVEN THINK ABOUT SLIPPING AWAY!
WHY DID YOU EVEN LEAVE YOUR SHIP, SANA?! THIS ISN'T YOUR FIGHT!
I'M KEEPING AN EYE ON MY INVESTMENT!
SHOULDN'T WE BE MORE CONCERNED ABOUT WHAT THESE PEOPLE ARE RUNNING FRO--
RRROOOOHHHHRRRR

SHOOT IT!
BLASTERS ON'T WORK...
WHAT THE...
LOOK OUT!
≡COUGH COUGH≡ IS EVERYBODY ALL RIGHT?
SANA? WHERE'S SANA?
I SEE STORMTROOPERS UP AHEAD. WHICH MEANS WITHOUT WEAPONS, WE'RE IN BIG...
TWEET BADEEP BEEBOO
ARTOO? WHAT ARE YOU...
GREAT. NEXT SOME OLD WIZARD WILL BE TELLING ME TO USE THE FORCE.
ALWAYS WANTED TO TRY ONE OF THESE.
ALL RIGHT, PEOPLE, FOLLOW ME.

AND MAY THE FORCE BE WITH US.
WWWWWRRRRRRRRRHH
I'D SETTLE FOR A GOOD BLASTER.

LOOKS LIKE YOU'RE OUT OF A JOB, GAMEMASTER.
NOT EXACTLY. PUT DOWN THE SABER, KID.
I THOUGHT YOU WERE TRAINING ME TO FIGHT?
NO, I WAS TRAINING YOU TO *DIE.*
IT'S YOUR FAULT YOU MESSED THAT UP. IT'S JUST NOT YOUR LUCKY DAY, IS IT, KID?
IF IT WAS, YOU WOULD'VE HAD YOUR HEAD BITTEN OFF BY THAT MONSTER. INSTEAD...
...I GOTTA TAKE YOU IN.
TAKE ME IN?
I'M A ***STORMTROOPER,*** KID. VADER'S FIST.
WHICH MEANS THERE'S A CELL IN A STAR DESTROYER SOMEWHERE WITH YOUR NAME WRITTEN ALL OVER IT.
I'M AFRAID THE SAGA OF THE LAST JEDI WON'T BE ENDING WITH ANY MEMORABLE BANGS. MORE LIKE A TINY LITTLE WHIMP--

HGGH!
I WILL FEED YOU TO MY LIZARDS, YOU WRETCHED LITTLE MAN! AND THEN FEED THOSE LIZARDS TO A BIGGER LIZARD!
AND THEN HAVE THAT LIZARD BARBECUED!
HGGGHK!
YOU WILL DIE SCREAMING AND WEEPING, YOU...!
THE BOY! FIND THE BOY!
THE ONE WITH THE LIGHTSABER!
BUT... THEY'VE ALL GOT LIGHTSABERS!

THAT SABER DOESN'T LOOK HALF BAD ON YOU, HAN.
I'M JUST TRYING NOT TO CUT MY OWN FACE OFF. GOOD TO SEE YOU STILL IN ONE PIECE, LUKE.
YEAH, SORRY I DRAGGED YOU INTO MORE OF MY CRAZINESS.
BELIEVE ME, KID, YOUR TRIP CAN'T HAVE BEEN NEAR AS CRAZY AS MINE. YOU FIND WHAT YOU WERE LOOKING FOR AT LEAST?
I FOUND EVERYTHING I WAS LOOKING FOR, HAN. A WHOLE GIANT ROOM OF IT. JUST RIGHT UP--
ARTOO! YOU FOUND BEN'S JOURNAL!
QUICK, SHOW ME THE WAY TO THE--
A BOOK? ALL THIS FOR A BOOK?
NO, THERE'S SO MUCH MORE IN GRAKKUS'S MUSEUM. THE HOLOCRONS, ALL THE JEDI TEACHINGS...WE JUST HAVE TO GO...
REINFORCEMENTS. AND THEIR BLASTERS ACTUALLY WORK.
CHEWIE, TAKE LUKE OUTTA HERE.
NO! I HAVE TO--
GO! I'LL FIND LEIA AND...
LEIA?

IF YOU'RE GONNA KILL ME, AT LEAST MAKE IT QUICK.
DON'T MOVE OR I MIGHT. I'M NOT SO GOOD WITH THIS THING.
YOU CAME BACK FOR ME, AFTER EVERYTHING I...
NOW WHAT WOULD HAN SAY IF I LEFT HIS LOVING WIFE TO DIE ON NAR SHADDAA? C'MON, MRS. SOLO. LET'S GET YOU OUT OF HERE.
NOT... SOLO. NOT...
NAME'S... SANA STARROS. I'M NOT...
I'M NOT REALLY HIS WIFE.

MARRIAGE WAS A SCAM. PART OF A ROBBERY. WENT SOUR. HAN TOOK OFF...WITH MY CUT.
BEEN LOOKING FOR HIM...TO GET WHAT'S COMING TO ME.
LOOKS LIKE I FINALLY DID.
SO WHAT YOU'RE TELLING ME IS...WE SHOULD PROBABLY RENEGOTIATE OUR DEAL.
MIGHT AS WELL DROP ME HERE THEN. IF I'M ALIVE, I'M NOT LEAVING TILL I GET WHAT'S MINE. NEED THAT MONEY...NEED IT TO...
JUST PROMISE ME YOU WON'T GET HAN KILLED BEFORE I GET PAID.
RIGHT NOW, I CAN'T PROMISE YOU I WON'T GET US KILLED.
THINGS ARE DEFINITELY R BORING WHEN YOU'RE ROUND, PRINCESS. I'M ARTING TO SEE WHAT HE LIKES ABOUT...
ARRGGHH.
LESS TALKING, MORE RUNNING, SANA STARROS.
AYE AYE, YOUR HIGHNESS.

"IT WOULD APPEAR YOUR MISSION WAS A SUCCESS.
"THE HUTT WILL BE OF MUCH USE TO US."
HE HELPED US RID THE GALAXY OF MORE SCATTERED TRACES OF THE JEDI. THE EMPEROR WILL BE PLEASED.
THOUGH IT SEEMS THE GREATEST PRIZE ELUDED US.
I'M AFRAID SO. THE BOY ESCAPED.
WHAT DID YOU LEARN OF THIS BOY?
BUT PUT ME BACK IN THE FIELD, SIR, AND I PROMISE YOU I'LL MAKE UP FOR--
DID HE HAPPEN TO MENTION...HIS NAME?
NO, MY LORD, HE DID NOT.
ALL I KNOW IS THAT HE IS YOUNG AND UNTRAINED. MORE BRAVE THAN WISE. AND NOT WITHOUT GIFTS.
HE'S NOT A JEDI. NOT YET. BUT GIVEN TIME...
GIVEN TIME... HE WILL BE CRUSHED. JUST LIKE THE REST OF THE REBELLION.
TELL ME WHAT ELSE YOU LEARNED OF THIS BOY, SERGEANT KREEL.

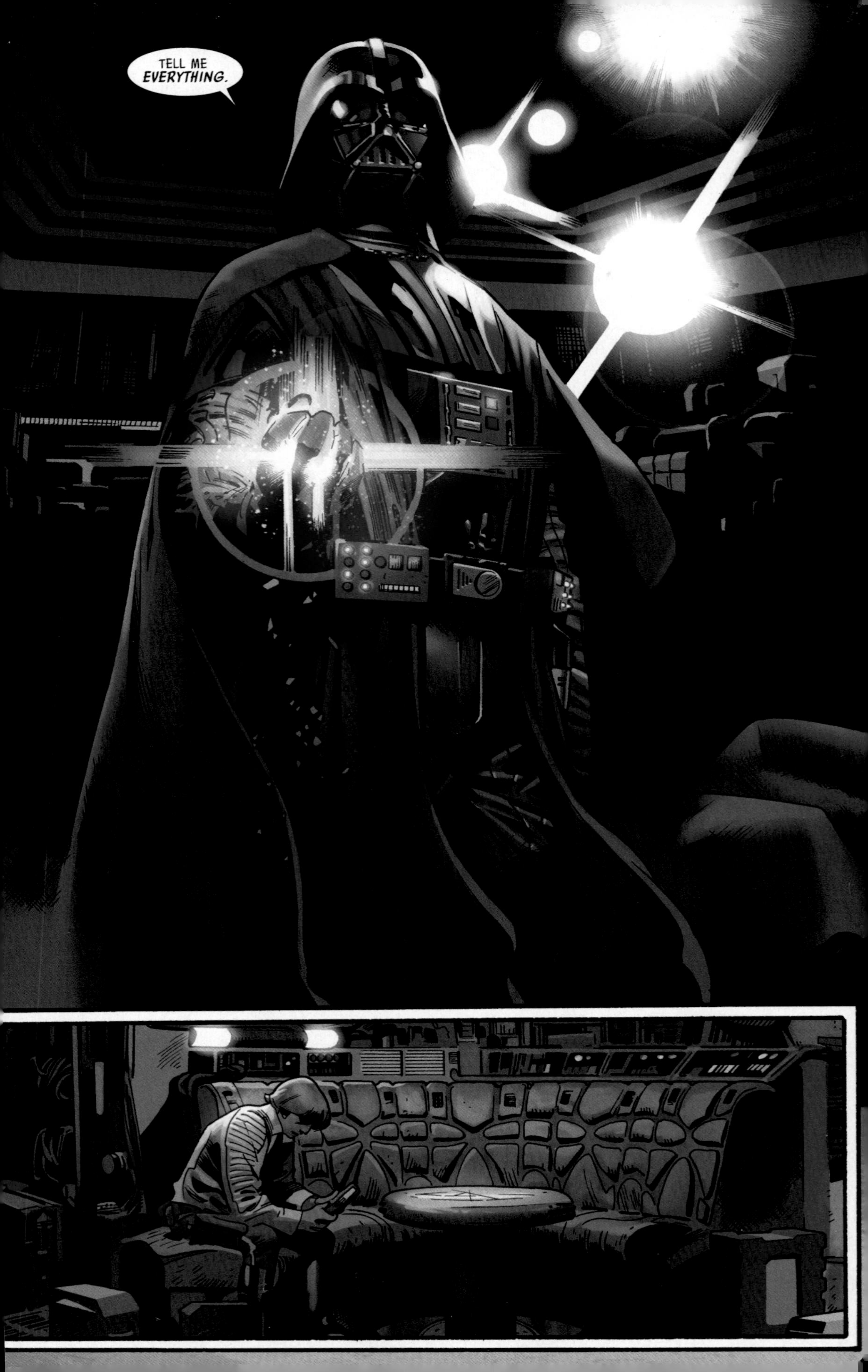
TELL ME *EVERYTHING.*

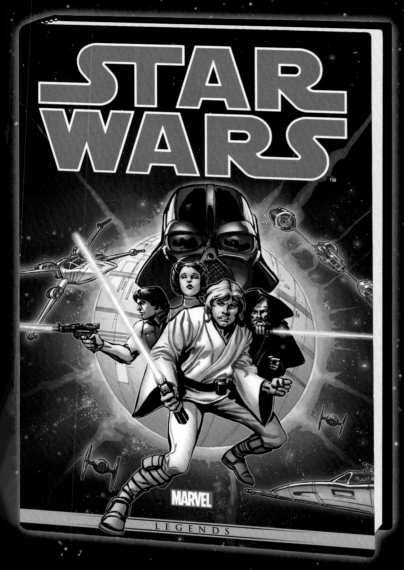

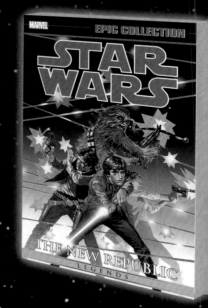